T0049833

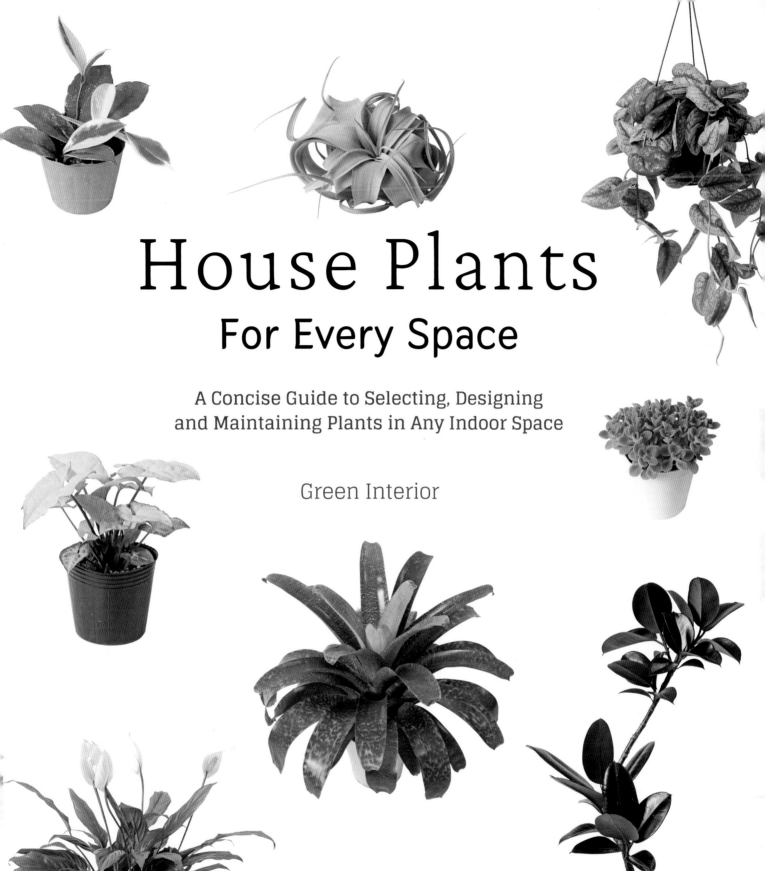

House Plants

For Every Space

A Concise Guide to Selecting, Designing
and Maintaining Plants in Any Indoor Space

Green Interior

TUTTLE Publishing

Tokyo | Rutland, Vermont | Singapore

CONTENTS

PART 3 A House Plant Catalog

PART 4 Living with House Plants

Why We Wrote This Book

As our lifestyles diversify, the ways we spend time at home and in the workplace environment are changing little by little. And with these changes, more and more people are wanting to try growing plants in each environment. It's great that there are so many new people interested in plants. Plants give us so much, but what we want to convey most of all is how they enrich and color our daily lives. They are there to greet us in the morning when we rise and when we return home later in the day. On days off, spending more time with them than usual allows us to appreciate their changes and sense the changing of the seasons through their new buds or blossoms. Time spent caring for them feels like a little luxury.

As plants are living creatures, cultivating them does take some knowledge, but once you have the key points, it's really pretty simple. We've compiled these kinds of "how-tos" with actual examples of living with plants—and of many plant varieties—to illustrate the basic points. We hope this book will lead to encounters with new plants, and to an everyday life that feels a bit more enriched.

—House Plant Specialists Green Interior
(Mashita Etsuhiro and Sato Momoko)

PART 1

House Plants as Décor

This is a collection of examples of indoor greenery that we cultivate at Green Interior. Here, we present foliage plants growing vigorously in various rooms. Tricks behind the methods of display and so on are also given, so before you start working foliage plants into your lifestyle, take a look to get your imagination going. You're sure to find your ideal room.

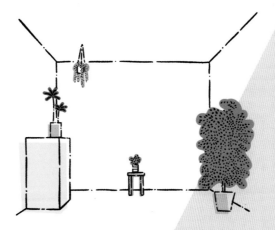

Why Do We Love Green So Much?

▶ S RESIDENCE

The owners of S Residence came to us for advice on indoor and outdoor plants when they began building their home. There are various plants in every room. Mr. S came to our store quite often, increasing his plant varieties and his knowledge about cultivation little by little. He says that plants have become his family's life work. In the living room, a huge, wild *Ficus irregularis* sp2 complements the high ceiling. We used cement-type pots to fit in with the interior. In areas where large beams were installed in order to display plants, we hung large, heavy plants.

(From left) Platycerium elephantotis, Ficus irregularis sp2, Euphorbia oncoclada f. crist, Ficus benjamina

Neoregelia (above, made into a kokedama moss ball), Begonia maculata (at back), Dyckia (two in front)

A Rhipsalis ramulosa adds color to the staircase

Ferns and other leafy plants sit at the base of a large Tabebuia, *Alocasia odora* and *Dracaena reflexa* in the jungle-like room of the H residence. Various plants are positioned to create differences in height. One technique is to use hanging plants in place of a curtain to block the line of sight. Sun-loving woody plants and cacti are positioned by the window in the bright living room on the second floor, with Araceae —which like weak light—further inside, taking the environment in which each plant grows best into consideration in order to position them. "Sitting here gazing at the plants while enjoying a drink is a great way to relax," says Mr. H.

Tabebuia (left), with a Ficus panda var. grandiflora spreading out wide at its side. At their base is a N. exaltata 'Teddy Junior' and a Epipremnum aureum (devil's ivy)

INTERIOR 2

Welcome to the Jungle

▶ H RESIDENCE

Greenery that Grows Alongside Your Family

▶ U RESIDENCE

The lively family composition of the U Residence is made up of a couple, small children and two dogs. The plants are displayed mainly on the kitchen counter and ornamental shelves, out of reach of the mischievous children. Mrs. U loves decorating and decided to use plants to finish off the free-standing house that they had been so particular about. In response to her request for stylish, healthy plants that are beginner-friendly, we selected types with clear care methods. The daily care of the plants and looking across kitchen greenery at her family in the open-plan living space make Mrs. U happy.

Sansevieria zeylanica is positioned in the entrance hall to catch the bright morning light

INTERIOR 4

INTERIOR 5

INTERIOR 6

INTERIOR 7

INTERIOR 8

INTERIOR 9

Displaying Symbolic Greenery

| INTERIOR 4 | ▶ T RESIDENCE

The large, bright dining room is surrounded by windows. The airy, large-growing *Pithecellobium congertum* (Everfresh tree) is just right for a large space. We used a washgray pot cover that works well with white and wood so that the plant would complement the rest of the décor.

| INTERIOR 6 | ▶ F RESIDENCE

The leaves of the *Hyophorbe lagenicaulis* (bottle palm) spread out to the sides as it grows, with some extending towards the window and others towards the television unit, on which a Ficus macrocarpa and Sansevieria are placed. We recommend positioning small pots on a sideboard, as it is easy to incorporate them there.

| INTERIOR 8 | ▶ S RESIDENCE

Mr. S needed plants to suit the ends of shelves. With its wild, thick trunk, the *Beaucarnea recurvata* (ponytail palm) was a perfect choice. The jute coffee bag used as a pot cover lends a casual look and enhances enjoyment.

| INTERIOR 5 | ▶ E RESIDENCE

Used as a main tree at the E Residence, the *Schefflera Chiang Mai* has fresh, light green leaves that suit the pastel blue of the feature wall. It's a large type, but still with about a foot (30 cm) of space before it reaches the ceiling, so its owner can enjoy the gradual changes in its branching as it grows.

| INTERIOR 7 | ▶ K RESIDENCE

The *Monstera deliciosa* is known for its unique leaf formation, and makes its presence felt even when placed on a shelf in a small pot. The matte gold pot cover works well with the existing interior décor, and the image of the plant in the mirror is also attractive.

| INTERIOR 9 | ▶ T RESIDENCE

The vibrant mottling of the *Pachira glabra* 'Milky Way' brightens up a room. The gentle wave in the trunk is a unique feature devised by this particular grower. The unique plants and pared-back décor create a striking dining room.

A Breath of Life in an Industrial Setting

▶ S RESIDENCE

Built next to the river, this house incorporates views of nature into daily life. Commencing with the main tree to bring plants into the house, the residents were charmed by its style and the pleasure in cultivating it, and the indoor space is now full of plants. They have increased their collection, taking time selecting plant stock that move them. As the second floor living area has many windows and plenty of space that receives sunlight, they have placed many succulents there, as these plants prefer bright places. Husband S's hobby is unusual plants in small pots. Key to this décor is the fact that the plants have been repotted into cement pots to blend into the industrial-style interior.

From left: Cereus hildmannianus cv. nuda, Euphorbia maharaja, Tillandsia xerographica, Schefflera

From left: Alluaudia procera, Tephrocacutus articulatus v.inermis, Euphorbia debilispina, Cereus, Euphorbia lactea 'White Ghost'

From left: Trichocaulon annulatum, Opuntioideae (two), Euphorbia horrida, Sansevieria Pinguicula, Adenium arabicum

Into the Woods

▶ S RESIDENCE

The lively S Residence, where many plants jostle by the window. Lightweight plants are suspended from the ceiling by means of tools specifically for this purpose. The trick to this sort of display is to adjust the length of the hanging rod and create space between the plants hanging on it, which also serves to make sure that the leaves do not overlap and air can circulate. Mr. S has brought home small plant stock and raised them to become large, magnificent specimens through his careful maintenance. In this room, one can sense his love for plants.

Example of a Large Plant

▶ K RESIDENCE

Mr. K is involved in architectural design. We chose an oversized *Strelitzia nicolai* with large leaves as the main plant for the garage apartment, which retains the materiality of the matte black steel frame. The small pots and hanging plants are arranged to blend into the interior, and Mr. K says he enjoys seeing their appearance change depending on the time of day. It's a space that is dedicated to the pursuit of greenery as décor.

Where Animals and Plants Coexist

Mr. S loves living creatures; his main lifework is caring for his plants and pets. He regularly visits our store to carefully select plants to increase his collection and says with a smile that he enjoys the time every week when he waters and maintains all his plants in one go. In order to keep plants on the floor out of reach of his dog, he places them on stands in smooth ceramic pots. With hanging pots decorating the sunlit window area, the living room is a lively space.

▶ S RESIDENCE

While Being Gazed at by Greenery...

▶ A RESIDENCE

Mr. A began placing plants in his dining room with large windows. When working from home, this is the room he uses. The family tends to use this table for most things, creating a peaceful space for the family to gather.

| INTERIOR 15 |

This is My Solution

▶ M RESIDENCE

When this couple were planning a home where they could both easily spend time, Mr. M was imagining incorporating plants from the design stage. Once they'd moved in, they chose plants together, ranging from small to large sizes. The photo shows the working space in the bedroom, where the husband's plant choices are lined up.

When reclining on the sofa in this resort-like living room, it's as if one's view is veiled by large leaves. The deep green of the *Strelitzia nicolai*'s glossy leaves works well with the chic black foundation of the modern interior.

| INTERIOR 16 |

A Single Plant Makes a Big Difference!

▶ O RESIDENCE

| INTERIOR 17 |

Only as Much Green as Needed

▶ C RESIDENCE

On the side table sits a *Ficus benjamina barok* with its characteristically curly leaves. The pot cover is in a stylish cement material. Mr. C is growing his collection of favorites little by little. He says his friends like the plants too, and he enjoys growing them.

Life and Plants, Me and You

▶ S RESIDENCE

This is the home of Ms. Sato, the store manager at Green Interior. As the living room doesn't get much sunlight, she focuses mainly on plant varieties that can grow even in shade, and enjoys rotating them with the plants from the sunny second floor. People often ask if having a lot of pots makes care a chore, but she has chosen types that don't need frequent watering, allowing for stress-free cultivation regardless of her work schedule. As long as they get a look-in at least once a week, the plants are fine. The use of stools and shelves allows for the creation of height differences the display.

From left: Rhipsalis, Aeschynanthus, Epipremnum aureum, Aglaomorpha coronans, Beaucarnea recurvata, Rhipsalis, Monstera adansonii etc

From left: Dracaena reflexa cv. Song of Jamaica, Hoya caudata, Ficus benjamina barok, Euphorbia platycada, Euphorbia lactea 'White Ghost', Anthurium, Monstera, Calatheas

From left: Vriesea, Aromaticus, Euphorbia tirucalli etc

From left: Spring flowers such as cherry blossoms, hyacinths and tulips

From left: Ivy and cactus, along with cut flowers and dried arrangements

| INTERIOR 19 |

The Right Answers for Green as Décor

▶ **N RESIDENCE**

When building their free-standing house, the owners welcomed two types of Ficus as the main and sub trees, slowly adding pot plants into the bedroom, entrance hall and so on as they became more accustomed to having plants. Mr. N says they enjoy experiencing the daily growth and the changing of the seasons through their plants, including seasonal cut flowers. The plants have comfortably blended into the natural-looking décor of the space, with the size and positioning of each plant selected to complement other plants and small objects. The small pots by the little window in the kitchen are lovely.

PART 2

How to Choose & Display Plants

When starting to use plants as décor, it's important to decide first of all which plants to choose and where to place them. Carefully considering this starting point is key for living with plants. This chapter summarizes how to choose and display your very first house plant. Read this before purchasing plants and then head out to find ones that suit you.

How Should I Choose My First Your Plant?

It's extremely tricky choosing a favorite first house plant from the huge variety of foliage plants. Many people want to start with something small, but in actual fact, an established plant in a large pot is robust and easy to grow, with less fear of failure. These are the three main things to consider when choosing your first plant.

Start by thinking about where the plant will be positioned

Positioning for house plants must meet these four conditions: receiving sunlight, receiving airflow, a temperature of more than 50 °F/10 °C (apart from overnight) and not in the line of breeze from an air conditioner. Often, rooms such as the living room, kitchen or bedroom where one tends to spend a long time are suitable and provide an environment where it is easy to grow plants. Sunlight is essential in order for plants to carry out the photosynthesis that creates the energy they need to live. Airflow is vital for the promotion of new buds and healthy growth, along with preventing pest infestations. Furthermore, many ornamental plants originate from environments with high temperatures and humidity, so will not grow well if kept outdoors or in cold places. Additionally, the breeze from air conditioners damages leaves by making them cold and dry, and should therefore be avoided. On top of these considerations, take a look around the room where you plan to place the plant and check whether the spot you want to use will be favorable for its health. If you already have furniture and so on positioned in the room, you may need to completely change the layout to create ideal positioning for the plant.

Woody "treelike" types and herbaceous "leafy" types

House plants can broadly be divided into types according to appearance: woody, "treelike" types with leaves growing from thick branches, and "leafy" herbaceous types and succulents, which have leaves and stems as the plant's main parts. Deciding on your preferred look of a plant before you select one makes it easier to choose from the large variety of decorative plants.

Choosing a variety that's easy to grow

The keywords here are "infrequent watering" and "I think I've heard of this plant." Plants whose names sound familiar are generally common or at least well-known, and tend to be robust. Examples include rubber plants, yucca, Pachira and Dracaena.

Choosing a Guardian Tree

In Japanese gardening, whether indoors or out, it's customary to choose a tree or large plant as a symbol or, if kept outside the door, a "guardian" of the home. Large plants have the advantage of being robust and relatively easy to tend because many of them are mature. If placing the plant indoors, consider what kind of plant will work and in which position—have fun visualizing different possibilities as you select the plant that's right for you.

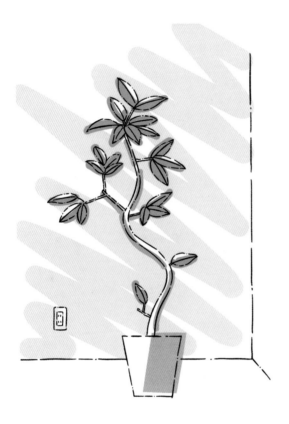

What kinds of plants are there?

When it comes to plants taller than 60″ (150 cm) that can be used as symbol trees, the individual plants sold have a presence that recalls their place of origin, with thick trunks and strong aerial roots, large, spreading leaves and so on. *Benghalensis, umbellata, benjamina* and other easy-to-cultivate varieties of Ficus are popular with everyone from beginners to advanced growers, and it's possible to choose from various tree shapes such as those which have been curved or trained to "flow" a certain way (see p38). There are also varieties that are not readily available in small pots, such as breadfruit and cinnamon trees. It can be said that some plants such as Dracaena and Schefflera, which are admired for their rough bark and unique form, palm varieties and Strelitzia with large outspread leaves and so on, can only be appreciated at large sizes. Monstera, cacti and so on that are woody and whose roots grow above the ground also have many fans and are widely enjoyed. It's a real thrill finding a large-sized plant that suits your taste from the various unique types on offer.

Slim? Voluminous?

It's fine to choose a plant that is slim and won't take up too much space in a room, but it's also great to select something with more volume. Positioned near the sofa or in the center of the living or dining room, the plant will have a stronger sense of presence.

Regenerate plants to ensure growth

During the growth period from spring to summer, prune old leaves and branches that have grown (see p90) in order to regenerate plants. If cultivated without pruning, plants will not bud properly and will lose their form, becoming misshapen. The key is to neaten their form and encourage new buds through pruning.

Choosing a Plant the Right Size for Your Table

In comparison with large plants, small plants have the advantage of blending in with the décor, even if their form is unique. However, being in a small pot can create harsh conditions for plants. Careful maintenance is the secret to being able to enjoy them over a long period.

What kinds of plants are there?

There is a wealth of varieties of plants that are the right size for displaying on the table. It's easy to enjoy standard types, unusual, hard-to-find varieties, those with interesting shapes and so on. Readily available woody types include Ficus varieties such as *macrocarpa* and *pumila*, along with Croton, Schefflera, Pachira and Dracaena varieties such as *concinna*. Among herbaceous types, *Epipremnum aureum*, Peperomia and Calatheas are popular, while there are a lot of unique succulents such as cacti, Sansevieria, Haworthia and Euphorbia. As there are so many types of succulent, it's good to build up a collection little by little. Even if they have uniquely patterned leaves and shapes, they are small in size, so they can be boldly work them into the décor. Furthermore, seedlings germinated from seeds are also available in this size range. Seedlings grow strong and robust, and the plant's individuality can be clearly seen.

How to grow small plants well

Leaves are lush

Thick trunk

Start by choosing plant stock that is firm and thick. In human terms, plants that are the right size for the table are still children. In comparison with large plants, they are not strong, so try to choose the best stock possible. The key is to observe the plant carefully and make sure not to miss any changes in its condition.

Things to watch out for when cultivating

The soil in small pots dries out easily, so pay attention to plants running out of water. Choosing dry-loving types for display on shelves or as hanging pots that take some effort to water, and positioning water-loving types in the kitchen, bathroom or other places where watering is easy makes maintenance simple.

Choosing a Succulent or Cactus

Due to the innate qualities of succulents, apart from pots, it's possible to plant them in mugs or deep dishes, so they are perfect to display as interior décor. Furthermore, they come in a wide range of shapes and sizes, some low-key and others with a strong sense of presence. There are rare varieties among them, so creating a collection is one way to enjoy them.

What exactly are succulents?

Plants that can store water in their stems and leaves are called succulents. Their appearance is generally fleshy, indicating an abundance of moisture, as their stems and leaves are characteristically thick and plump. Most types grow in places where the rainy and dry seasons are clearly delineated, and it is thought that they have developed to be able to store water within their physical structure in order to survive dry seasons. They are popular as they need infrequent watering and are easy to grow. Succulents are often divided into "cacti" and "other succulents," and small cacti can often be found in home centers or variety stores. There are various large types, such as column-shaped ones with no spines and families of spherical varieties. Apart from these, there are also Aloes, Sansevieria and many other families and varieties of succulents available with varying appearances. With cultivars being created all the time, these are plants that are highly collectible.

These are the kinds of places to put them

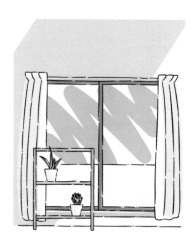

Succulents should be placed in the brightest, warmest place in the room. If placing them in a bay window or inside shelving, make sure that they regularly get some breeze, as lack of airflow damages the plant stock. Some types do not like the cold, so make sure they are not in cold drafts during winter.

Things to watch out for when cultivating

Although resilient against dryness, succulents wither if the soil dries out. Check soil once a week and add water if it has dried out. In order avoid damaging the plant stock, water in the cool of the evening during midsummer, and in midwinter use water at room temperature and water only moderately.

Choosing a Plant that Suits Your Lifestyle

Many people say that their plants end up dying. This may be just because the person and the plant are not a good match. Plants in pots will die if not cared for. Selecting plants that suit your lifestyle is an important point in order to grow them without difficulty.

Matching plants to your lifestyle

Having found your plant, you want it to live a long time without dying. Having said that, paying a lot of careful attention can be stressful. If you choose a plant to suit your lifestyle, it will be easy to grow and you will be able to care for it without difficulty. For example, for those whose lifestyle involves rising early and enjoying their morning activities, fern varieties that require frequent watering in the form of careful misting would suit. It can be incorporated into a pleasant start-of-day routine. For those who are often out due to work and so on, woody types and succulents that retain water well are a good choice. Shade-tolerant herbaceous varieties such as Monstera are a safe bet for people who often sleep with the curtains closed in the morning. Those who are often at home may get more enjoyment from *Pithecellobium congertum* (Everfresh) or Calatheas whose leaves open out during the day.

Choose a plant to suit your personality

For lazy people, hydroponics are a hassle-free way to tell when water is running low. Woody types with plenty of foliage or herbaceous types with large leaves suit those who want to spend a lot of time carefully tending plants. Removing leaves, nipping off the petioles and so on allows for a lot of maintenance.

Value your taste in plants' appearances

Liking the look of a plant is actually important. If you don't become attached to a plant, you will lose interest in it and fail to notice changes in its condition, in some cases even letting it die. As one's gaze orients towards things that one likes, it's easy to notice changes in a plant that you like and take appropriate measures to keep it healthy for a long time.

Selecting the Growing Medium

All plants need some type of growing medium, and there are many types to suit various needs (such as avoidance of direct touch, prevention of insects and so on), so choose the type that works for you.

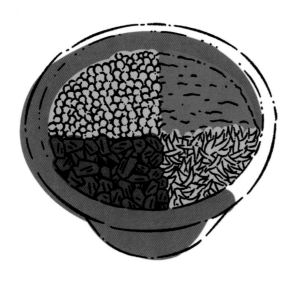

How many mediums are there?

Even taking only the typical materials into account, there is soil, sphagnum moss, sponges, horticultural soil made from processed wood chips, hydroculture mediums, charcoal and so on. The most common of these is still soil. Soil is suited to supporting heavy stems and leaves, and is used for most plants over a yard/meter tall. Commercially available soil contains organic matter and fertilizer, allowing it to store moisture and provide nutrients necessary for growth. Furthermore, changes in soil moisture levels are less pronounced than those in the air, meaning there is less stress on the plant with the seasonal changes in humidity. Hydroculture mediums and charcoal are used for hydroponics. Plant growth is not as fast as in soil, but the inorganic substances used keep insect infestations at bay and timing for watering is obvious, making them a popular option. Recently mediums in a lightweight sponge form that contain the same nutrients as soil have been developed, expanding the range of materials from which to choose.

Some materials prevent insects

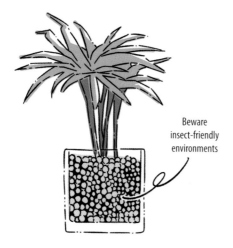

Beware insect-friendly environments

Insects that emerge from inside pots, such as small fruit flies and springtails, like places where there are nutrients. As sphagnum moss and hydroculture mediums are inorganic, they create environments that do not support such insects. If you're not well-placed to battle insects, consider giving these materials a try.

Choosing materials that can be displayed

Inorganic materials that allow plants to grow hydroponically are made in colors and shapes that allow them to blend in with the plants, so many of them are ideal for displaying as decor objects. Displaying them in clear glass, or growing them in water only, so as to show the roots, makes for a stylish look.

Choosing Plants Based on Tree or Leaf Shape

Plants come in many different shapes and have various shaped leaves. For instance, the impression made by a "natural tree form" which plays up the natural shape of a plant is completely different from that of a "bent tree form" that has intentionally been trained into a bent shape. The shape of a plant is important within the context of interior décor. There are many leaf shapes also, so visualize how a plant will look when displayed in order to select suitable varieties.

 Types of tree forms and their characteristics

Each type of tree form has various characteristics. Here are some typical examples of tree forms achieved by growers inducing growth or pruning back branches and leaves. Each type of tree form has various characteristics. Here are some typical examples of tree forms achieved by growers inducing growth or pruning back branches and leaves.

| Natural tree form | Bent tree form | Flowing tree form | Parasol form |

FICUS BENJAMINA VARIEGATA

A so-called "tree-like" tree form of the woody type. The tree form does not lose its shape much, and leaf or branch growth should be pruned about once every two years.

FICUS ALTISSIMA VARIEGATA

A tree form in which the trunk is curved into an S shape or spiral formation. The branches and leaves grow extending from the main trunk. It requires the same care as a plant with natural tree form.

SCHEFFLERA CHIANG MAI

A tree form in which the trunk is trained to flow out to the side. Pruning leaf and branch growth sticking up or out maintains the form of the plant.

PACHIRA

In this tree form, the leaves are concentrated at the top of the tree. If they spread out or grow too much, they are pruned, with the tree shape adjusted when new leaves emerge.

| Upright form | Fountain form | Fan form | Trailing form |

DRACAENA WARNECKII CV. LEMON LIME

A slim, straight-growing tree form with no width. If Dracaena varieties fill out too much, remove the bottom leaves and trim off any stock that is growing too densely.

SPATHIPHYLLUM 'MINI MERRY'

A tree form in which the leaves extend from the base to form a soft, fluffy look. Once the plant stock has grown, repot it into a larger pot.

STRELITZIA NICOLAI

A tree form in which the leaves extend boldly from the base. As they tend to spread out, if any of the outer leaves stick out, trim them off at the base.

AESCHYNANTHUS 'THAI PINK'

Creeping or vine plants that grow with their leaves trailing from the pot. Prune if the plant grows too long.

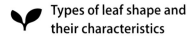 **Types of leaf shape and their characteristics**

There are also various types of leaf shape. As plants in the same family or genus tend to have similarly shaped leaves, choosing plants by their leaf shape lets you narrow down the species you prefer.

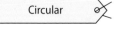 Circular

A completely round, cute shape. Common among small types and easy to handle. Displaying them at eye level height allows for greater appreciation of the leaf shape.

 Elliptical

A leaf shape often seen on woody type plants, they are on the large size and have a sense of presence. If the leaves start overlapping, prune to create gaps between them.

Ovoid

Common in Ficus varieties, these leaves create a natural impression. Size-wise, they vary from small to large.

 Lanceolate

A leaf form often seen on plants with large leaves such as herbaceous types. The pattern and coloration of the leaf vary widely depending on the species.

Needle or linear form

Characterized by long, elongated forms, these leaves are seen on palms and some narrow-leaf varieties of woody type plants. The clusters of fine leaves create a supple grass-like effect.

Sword-shaped

A long leaf shaped like a sword, with more width and thickness than the needle or linear form leaves. This is a common leaf shape in families such as Asparagaceae.

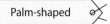 Palm-shaped

Resembles the palm of a human hand in shape. Seen in Schefflera varieties, Pachira and so on, where many leaves grow from branches to create volume.

Heart-shaped

Heart-shaped leaves are seen in Arums and varieties of Ficus. If leaves overlap or spread out, they should be pruned.

Arrowhead-shaped

Common in herbaceous species such as arums, these leaves grow in rosette formation to create a soft, airy tree form. There is a wide range of leaf colors and patterns.

Unique shape

Tree species with individualistic leaves that have large notches in them or are uniquely shaped. They are extremely popular for what they can bring to interior design.

Choosing a Pot

The sense of presence that pots and pot covers can contribute is also an important point for enjoying plants as décor items. There are many different types of pots to choose from in terms of appearance, but it is also important to consider whether you have chosen the right pot for the plant in the first place.

How to consider pots

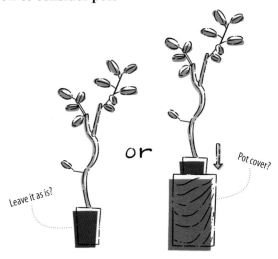

The vessel a plant is planted in is called a plant pot, and when indoors, a dish is placed beneath it to catch water from the pot. When displaying, you may either use the pot by itself or put it into a pot cover or planter, considering the plant type and size as well to choose something that works with the décor.

How do I choose the size of the pot?

In the case of plant pots, choose one that is the next size up from the original plant pot. Care is needed here, because if the pot is too large, it will be difficult for the roots to dry, leading to root damage and uneven root growth, which hinders plant growth. If using a pot cover, choose one the next size up from the pot. Be sure there will be room to fit your fingers or hands on either side of the pot edges.

Plant pot materials

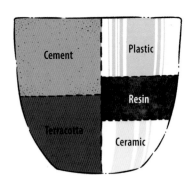

Plastic, resin and ceramic retain water well and are relatively light, making them popular choices. It is easy for the temperature to rise inside pots made from these materials so be on the lookout for root damage in the summer months. Cement and terracotta absorb moisture and are extremely breathable, so they suit plants that like dryness.

Pot cover materials and types

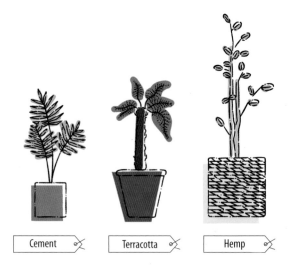

Generally, plants are sold in plastic pots. Pot covers come in various materials including ceramics, cement, terracotta, baskets, jute, hemp and fiberglass, so it's easy to choose one that suits your interior décor style.

Planter Guidelines

Go for industrial looks for a chic effect!

Cement pots are popular for their unrefined coolness. The pots themselves are subtle and so do not interfere with the presence of the plant. Key, too, is the fact that they blend in easily with interior décor.

Easy, stylish pot covers

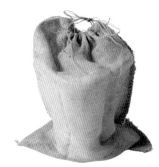

Even plants still in the plastic pots that they were purchased in become more stylish simply by placing them in pot covers like these. Many of them are comparatively cheap, and their appeal lies in their easy attainability.

Highly style-conscious, I like artisanal wares

Many handmade pots have unique designs. The plant and positioning must suit the pot and vice versa, so a sense of style is needed, but overall, these pots cannot be beaten as interior accents.

Cost performance first! Cheap is great!

Pots can be purchased even at places like dollar stores. There are lots of designs, so choose something to suit the plant. They break relatively easily, but as they cost very little, it's worth giving them a try.

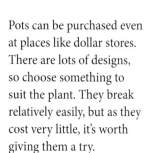

Staying Green Throughout the Year

SPRING April–June

Spring is the time for growth.
Great care must be taken in this period.

As temperatures rise and it gets warmer, roots activate and plants enter their growth period. They are at their strongest at this time and the stable temperatures make it the season for care and maintenance. Repotting, dividing stock, pruning and fertilizing are all carried out in this period. If soil is running low or the pot is getting too small for the plant, repot it (see p88), refresh soil, divide stock and so on. Prune leaves and branches that are getting too dense (see p90) and give the plant fertilizer to induce plenty of new buds. When many new buds emerge, leaves in dense sections, the outer parts of the plant and the lower parts of branches may turn yellow, but this is a metabolic process so there is no need to worry. Furthermore, if the plant flowers and those flowers remain for a prolonged period, the plant will lose its strength, so pick them off as soon as possible.

SUMMER July–August

Heat is the enemy in summer.
Watch out for leaf burn and root damage!

Ornamental plants are seemingly adept at coping with heat, but when kept indoors, where—unlike in nature—air does not circulate well, they can suffer root and leaf damage from heat and stuffy conditions, so care Is needed. Placing them outdoors or by a window that is not shaded by a curtain are big no-nos. Be careful to make sure they get a breeze and receive sunlight through a thin curtain. Leaves that suffer leaf burn lose their color, turning yellow or brown. If the plant suffers leaf burn, prune off only those leaves that are affected. In plant pots made from plastic, ceramic and other materials that retain water well, it is difficult for heat to escape in high temperatures, and roots may become damaged. Take measures against this by using pot covers and moving the plants somewhere that won't get too much sunlight. Limp, drooping branches and leaves are a sign that root damage has occurred.

In many places, the four seasons are very distinct. The growth of plants varies according to the season, so it's necessary to slightly alter care and the growing environment. Here, we look at plants' appearances and weak points over the four seasons.

FALL
September–November

Plants are easy to cultivate in fall. Their growth period slowly comes to an end.

The lingering summer heat at the start of fall makes it a season in which plants grow easily. Make sure they get some air circulating around them and stimulate their metabolism. For good plant stock that is putting out new foliage and is firm around the base, it is possible to repot to the next pot size and also do a little pruning. It's also a good idea to carry out maintenance on pots whose roots, branches and leaves became overgrown before summer. If you forgot to fertilize plants in spring, this is a good time to do it. For varieties that are sensitive to the cold, move them slightly away from windows to make sure that they are not affected by cold air from outside. Once the temperature drops, soil takes longer to dry out, so lessen the frequency of watering. Make sure not to water as often as you would in midsummer. Furthermore, the symptoms of roots damaged during the heat of summer may begin to appear during this period. Carefully observe the condition of plants as you care for them.

WINTER
Dec–March

Position plants in the brightest, warmest place possible in winter

The cold winter is a harsh season for plants. Bring them inside and position them in the brightest, warmest place possible. Move pots that have been placed near windows where cold air can easily enter, bringing them deeper into the room. Cold can cause leaf burn and root damage, so make sure not to place plants outside. Some plants can be burnt by cold even in just 10 minutes of watering. Symptoms of cold burn include wrinkled leaves, color disappearing from some sections of the plant, color changing to brown or black and so on. Remove leaves affected by leaf burn, but make sure about two-thirds of the plant's foliage remains. Make sure also to water using water at normal temperature*. Take a break from other maintenance.

*If used straight from the faucet in winter, water may be too cold, so let it sit for a little while to reach its regular temperature.

Displaying Plants to Highlight Their Charms

You've chosen a plant that you like and decided on the pot too! Now, the last consideration is how to display it. While it depends on the location of the room, here are some tips on how to display plants. The look of plants changes depending on how they are displayed. Visualize what sort of décor you would like in order to decide on the display.

Try grouping pots of the same type

Grouping together pots of the same color, material, shape, size etc. creates a sense of unity that allows plants to blend in with the overall look. For example, if pots are a uniform gray as shown above, even plants of different shapes and forms can be accommodated without appearing to fight one another for attention.

Display plants at different heights

If placing various plants within a room, try to make a point of displaying them at different heights. This creates texture and depth like that of a forest in nature, forming a space that is natural and has a sense of dimension. Try incorporating items such as stools, boxes and so on.

Make use of ornamental shelving

Try displaying trailing plants or types with unique forms on ornamental shelving. You can even try making your own shelving. It's easy to obtain materials at home centers or on the internet. Be particular about the designs of the pots being placed on the shelving too.

Try hanging plants

Hang hanging pot plants from high places. As hanging pots will be at a point higher than eye level, they have a presence that can be enjoyed differently from pots placed on a surface. Use mounting hardware to hang plants from beams and ceiling joists.

PART 3

A House Plant Catalog

Here, we present popular plant varieties that can be bought in stores, arranged by plant family. Photographs of the varieties show characteristics of that family in close-up. Even when grouped into families, there are all kinds of varieties, and plants take on different appearances depending on the season, so take your time to find the plants that you like. You may just encounter plants that exceed your expectations!

Moraceae

Moraceae is a typically tree-like family of plants that develop foliage on their branches. The so-called rubber tree types belonging to the fig genus are the main types, many of which have ovoid or elliptical leaves, with trunks of various colors. The wide range of sizes and shapes produced is also characteristic. When pruned, a rubbery sap emerges. There are also many types with unique tree forms due to their aerial roots (roots that extend above ground). The umbellata is vulnerable to cold and may lose its leaves in winter, but it produces many new buds in spring, forming thick foliage.

Ficus altissima variegata
Country of origin: India, Myanmar

Ficus African Prince
Country of origin: South Africa

Ficus altissima variegata

Benghalensis
Country of origin: India, Sri Lanka

Umbellata
Country of origin: Tropical Africa

Ficus irregularis sp2
Country of origin: Cultivar (South-east Asia, Polynesia)

Ficus benjamina variegata
Country of origin: Cultivar (India to South-east Asia)

Breadfruit
Country of origin: New Guinea, Maluku Islands

Ficus benjamina barok
Country of origin: Cultivar (India to South-east Asia)

Ficus burgundy
Country of origin: Cultivar (Tropical Asia)

Ficus benjamina
Country of origin: (India to South-east Asia)

Ficus jumbo leaf
Country of origin: Cultivar (Tropical Asia)

Ficus panda var. grandiflora
Country of origin:
Tropical America

Ficus rubiginosa
Country of origin: Australia

Ficus macrocarpa
Country of origin:
Japan, South-east Asia,
Taiwan, Australia

Arecaceae

With their wild-looking trunks and fine leaves, plants in the Palm family are popular, with a single tree bringing a sense of presence to interior spaces. The only way to propagate *Phoenix roebelenii*, a typical species, is by growing seedlings from seed. These trees are very enduring, living for more than 200 years. As they are sold with the roots exposed, careful watering is crucial. Unless grown from a seedling, the base of *Hyophorbe lagenicaulis* will not swell. In order to keep the foliage overall looking neat on this plant, it's best to limit it to two and a half fronds. Once the new buds develop from spring to summer, prune off any yellowed old leaves.

Phoenix roebelenii

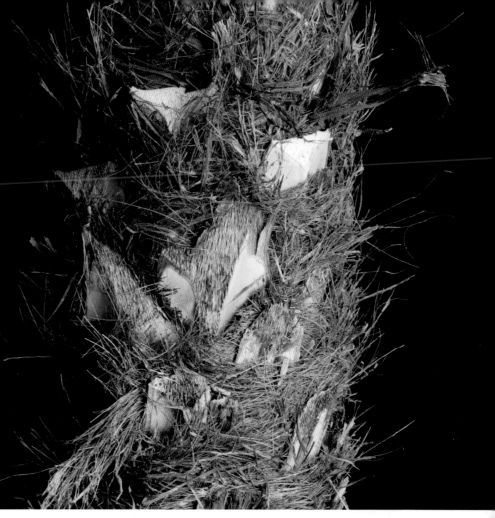

Phoenix roebelenii
Country of origin: Indochina

Hyophorbe lagenicaulis
Country of origin: Mascarene Islands

TYPE: TREES

Myrtaceae

Found natively mainly from south-east Asia to Australia and in South America, in Japan most plants in this family are treated as fruit trees for outdoor plantings. A typical house plant, *Syzygium cumini* is characterized by the white bark of its trunk and its soft leaves. It's often seen in its natural tree form and can be displayed to create a natural impression. It is popular for the look it creates when the leaves grow and begin to hang down. It is known as Amazon Olive, but it is completely unrelated to a regular olive, and is close to eucalypts, which are in the same Myrtaceae family. It does not cope with dry air conditions, so care for it by misting it with a spray bottle.

Syzygium cumini
Country of origin: South-east Asia

Pachira
Country of origin: Central to South America

Pachira glabra 'Milky Way'
Country of origin: (Central to South America)

Malvaceae

Resistant to dryness, this species is easy to care for. Popular for its ease of cultivation, the Pachira in recent years has attracted attention for the camouflage-pattern leaves of the Milky Way variety seedlings. As particular characteristics emerge strongly in seedlings, they do not revert to the green leaves of the ancestral plant. Most available stock has been grafted onto Pachira, and actual Milky Way seedlings are rare. It's common for the plants to be trained with the foliage concentrated at the top, but if growth is left unchecked it becomes messy and starts to hang down, so prune off branch and leaf growth in the spring to maintain the shape.

Apocynaceae

Native to arid regions, this family is characterized by its lumpy, enlarged roots and stems. It stores water in order to be able to survive in a dry environment. Known as tuberous plants, varieties with these looks are popular. This family is at its best in the warm periods when the unique plant stock flowers. In particular, the Adenium is known as the "rose of the desert" and its large, vibrant blooms are magnificent. Care for it in a warm spot that gets good sunlight and where air circulates. In winter, it sheds its leaves and is dormant, so reduce watering at that time.

Pachypodium rosulatum
Country of origin: Madagascar

Adenium arabicum
Country of origin: Arabian peninsula

Country of origin: Arabian peninsula

TYPE: TREES

Hypericaceae

A typical house plant from this family, Clusia is defined by its fleshy leaves and resilience against dryness. The pot plants available on the market are green all over, but as they grow they lignify and turn into large trees. If the surface of a leaf is scraped with a sharp instrument, the mark remains, meaning characters and images can be drawn on the leaves, and in the places it grows it is called the "message leaf" or "autograph tree". When ripe, the fruit opens into a rigid star shape and is used as an ornament in its native Hawaii.

Sterculiaceae

Due to the base of the swollen trunk resembling a wine bottle, Brachychiton are also called bottle trees. In their native environments they reach a height of as much as 22 yards (20 meters). They grow in a cycle during which they store water at the base of their roots from spring to summer in order to get through the dry winter period, so watering should be kept to a minimum over winter. Brachychiton produce new shoots vigorously during the growing season and sheds old leaves little by little as it grows, so it requires little pruning. When water is insufficient or the roots become clogged, the leaves turn yellow and drop off, making this variety easy to understand and care for.

※ Sterculiaceae is now transitioning to Malvaceae.

Brachychiton bidwillii
Country of origin: Australia

Brachychiton rupestris
Country of origin: Australia

Brachychiton rupestris

TYPE: TREES

Fabaceae

Small branches and soft leaves give plants in the Fabaceae family a soft, gentle appearance. "Ever fresh" grows vigorously from spring to fall, blossoming in spring with lantern-like flowers that hang down to create an enchanting appearance. Pods form from there and when they turn red, the seeds spill out. The leaves closing at night for the plant to rest is a sight to enjoy. The characteristic small leaves yellow and drop off if the soil gets too dry, so be sure to keep up with watering.

Sophora prostrata

Pithecellobium congertum "ever fresh"
Country of origin: South America

Sophora prostrata
Country of origin: Cultivar
(New Zealand)

TYPE: TREES

Asparagaceae

This is the wonderfully varied asparagus family. Some people may be familiar with plant names containing "Dracaena". The branches and leaves grow vertically, spreading little horizontally to create a slim tree shape. From spring to summer, new buds emerge from the inner edges of the leaves and the old leaves gradually die, leaving a tendon-like section that becomes part of the trunk. As they are resistant to dryness, they need infrequent watering and are easy to grow. Many plants in this family are vigorous and live for a long time, with some *Dracaena draco* trees confirmed to be up to 6000 years old.

Dracaena massangeana

Dracaena compacta
Country of origin: Cultivar (Tropical Africa)

Dracaena reflexa cv.Song of Jamaica
Country of origin: Cultivar (Tropical Asia, Tropical Africa)

Beaucarnea recurvata
Country of origin: South-east Mexico

Dracaena Warneckii cv. Lemon Lime
Country of origin: Cultivar (Tropical Africa)

Yucca elephantipes
Country of origin: North to Central America

Dracaena draco
Country of origin: Canary Islands

Dracaena marginata 'Rainbow'
Country of origin: Cultivar (Madagascar)

Dracaena cambodiana
Country of origin: South Asia,
Southern China

Dracaena warneckii gold ghost
Country of origin: Cultivar (Tropical Africa)

Cordyline stricta
Country of origin: Australia

Yucca desmetiana
Country of origin: Mexico

Dracaena reflexa
Country of origin: Cultivar (Tropical Asia, Tropical Africa)

Dracaena massangeana
Country of origin: Cultivar (Tropical Africa)

Cordyline sango
Country of origin: Cultivar (South-east Asia)

TYPE: TREES

Rubiaceae

Members if the Rubiaceae family have long been used in traditional medicine. One member that's loved as an ornamental is the coffee plant. It is characterized by its glossy leaves, with the pale green of the new buds creating a beautiful contrast with the deep green leaves in spring. When the plant grows to a height of more than a yard/meter and fills out, it has white flowers from spring to early summer and produces fruit as well. Fruiting takes nourishment from the plant, damaging the leaves and causing them to drop. If you want to enjoy the fruits, prune the leaves after harvesting to neaten the appearance. This plant is prone to cold, and if affected the leaves turn black and become damaged, so care for it in a warm place over winter.

TYPE: TREES

Araliaceae

Has leaves shaped like the palm of a hand, with the shape varying slightly between varieties. With its thick trunk and uniquely shaped branches, the Schefflera is so robust that it on Hachijojima, which is where it is produced in Japan, it is used as a windbreak. However it is vulnerable to moldering, so be aware of extremes in temperature and humidity, especially during midsummer. If it molders, the leaves and branches will turn black and droop. The Polyscias, with its soft leaves that grow trailing down, is called the Taiwan maple in its native land of Taiwan, and is popular as an auspicious charm that it said to bring wealth and honors.

Schefflera compacta

Polyscias fruticosa
Country of origin: India, South-east Asia, Polynesia

Schefflera Chiang Mai
Country of origin: Thailand

Hedera minister
Country of origin:
Cultivar (Europe, North Africa, West Asia)

Schefflera compacta
Country of origin: Cultivar (China, Taiwan)

Dizygotheca elegantissima
Country of origin: New Caledonia, Polynesia

Schefflera actinophylla
Country of origin: Australia, New Guinea

Schefflera
Country of origin: Taiwan, South China

Tupidanthus calyptratus
Country of origin: Assam, Malay Peninsula

TYPE: LEAFY PLANTS

Strelitziaceae

Characterized by the leaves that spread out boldly like a fan. From spring to summer, new buds emerge from the inner parts of the plant and open out into upright leaves, while in winter there is barely any activity. The old outer leaves eventually turn brown, so prune and neaten the plant in its spring growth period. If the plant stock matures in a warm environment it will produce flowers like a bird's crest. The flowers are white on the *Strelitzia nicolai*, while on the *reginae* they are orange and purple. The roots are fleshy and the plants are relatively resistant to dryness, making care easy, but the roots tend to grow well, so make sure to repot plants regularly.

Strelitzia nicolai

Strelitzia reginae
Country of origin: South Africa

Strelitzia nicolai
Country of origin: South Africa, Madagascar

Philodendron selloum

Dieffenbachia Tropic Snow

Philodendron selloum
Country of origin: Southern Brazil, Paraguay

Alocasia odora
Country of origin: Tropical Asia

TYPE: LEAFY PLANTS

Araceae

Having leaves with various markings and shapes and which come in a variety of colors, there are many popular herbaceous plants in the Araceae family. As there are many easy-to-cultivate varieties such as the Epipremnum and Anthurium, they are perfect for beginners who want to try growing something with a unique appearance. Types like the *Philodendron selloum* and Monstera have lots of aerial roots and trunks that rise in the same way as trees, allowing for full enjoyment of their growth process. Many types are vulnerable to cold, so care is needed during winter.

Monstera deliciosa
Country of origin: Mexico, Central America

Aglaonema commutatum 'Silver Queen'
Country of origin: Cultivar (Tropical Asia)

Spathiphyllum 'Mini Merry'
Country of origin: Tropical America

Dieffenbachia Tropic Snow
Country of origin: Cultivar (Colombia, Costa Rica)

Aglaonema Maria
Country of origin: Cultivar (Tropical Asia)

Epipremnum aureum 'Global Green'
Country of origin: Cultivar (Solomon Islands)

Monstera adansonii
Country of origin: Costa Rica

Schindapsus Treubii
Country of origin: Cultivar (Tropical Asia)

Anthurium andraeanum
Country of origin: Colombia

Philodendron birkin
Country of origin: Cultivar (Tropical America)

Syngonium podophyllum "White Butterfly"
Country of origin: Cultivar (Tropical America)

Alocasia Amazonica
Country of origin: Cultivar
(Tropical Asia)

TYPE: LEAFY PLANTS

Arecaceae

Characterized by fine needle-like or linear leaves, plants in this family have leaves of different lengths and shapes depending on their variety, with their standing forms varying also. They are popular for their cooling appearance. The ends of the leaves may brown and wither due to dryness in the air or soil in the dry indoor atmosphere during winter. Take care to prevent this through careful watering and misting. *Dypsis lutescens* transpires around a liter of water per day for its 2-yard /meter height, acting as a natural humidifier, and NASA research has proven that it can remove indoor toxins, so it is often used in offices and shops.

Howea forsteriana
Country of origin: Australia

Rhapis humilis
Country of origin: Southern China

Dypsis lutescens

Dypsis lutescens
Country of origin: Madagascar

Rhapis multifeda
Country of origin: Cultivar (Southern China)

Microcoelum weddelliana
Country of origin: Southern Brazil

Chamaedorea elegans
Country of origin: Mexico

Aeschynanthus Radicans Thai Pink
Country of origin: Tropical Asia

Esquinanthus Marmoratas
Country of origin: Tropical Asia

TYPE: LEAFY PLANTS

Gesneriaceae

Aeschynanthus is an ephiphytic plant that grows in tropical rainforests. The leaves are slightly fleshy and the stem of the plant lengthens as it grows in a vine-like fashion. The leaves take various shapes, such as round, fine and curled. Resistant to dryness, it is a variety often used in hanging pots. The main flowering period is from spring to summer, when the plant produces trumpet-shaped flowers of about 1½″ (3-4) cm in size in red or pink, which should be pinched off once they have finished blooming. When the leaves become too dense the withered leaves pile up around the base of the plant, so remove them regularly.

Aeschynanthus marmoratus

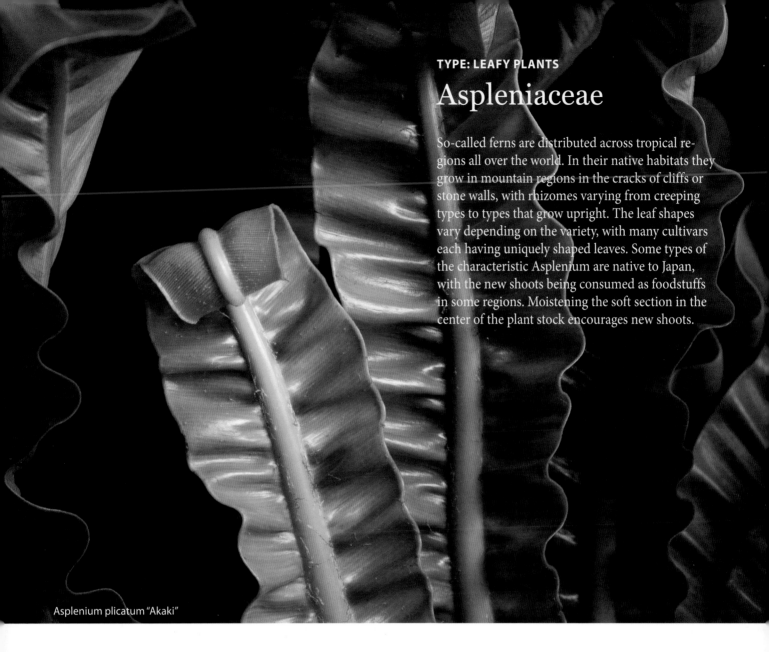

TYPE: LEAFY PLANTS
Aspleniaceae

So-called ferns are distributed across tropical regions all over the world. In their native habitats they grow in mountain regions in the cracks of cliffs or stone walls, with rhizomes varying from creeping types to types that grow upright. The leaf shapes vary depending on the variety, with many cultivars each having uniquely shaped leaves. Some types of the characteristic Asplenium are native to Japan, with the new shoots being consumed as foodstuffs in some regions. Moistening the soft section in the center of the plant stock encourages new shoots.

Asplenium plicatum "Akaki"

Asplenium hurricane
Country of origin: Cultivar

Asplenium plicatum "Akaki"
Country of origin: Cultivar

TYPE: LEAFY PLANTS

Bromeliaceae

Found natively mainly in the tropical and subtropical regions of the American continent, these plants are found in various places including forests, rocky areas and deserts. In order to adapt to their environments, their forms vary, with some collecting water in between their leaves to survive dry conditions and others growing soft hair on their leaves to absorb moisture and nutrients from the air efficiently. They grow slowly all year round. The Vriesea absorbs water from the ground and from the water storage part of its leaves, so can be cultivated by watering Its leaves, but in the cold period of winter the plant stock is easily damaged so water the soil only.

Vriesea fenestralis

Vriesea fenestralis
Country of origin: Brazil

Dyckia "brittle star"
Country of origin: Cultivar (South America)

Vriesea saundersii
Country of origin:
Central to South America

Dyckia Grand Marnier
Country of origin: Cultivar (South America)

Tillandsia seleriana
Country of origin: Central to South America

Tillandsia xerographica
Country of origin: Central to
South America

Apocynaceae

The foliage plants in the Apocynaceae family are popular for requiring little effort as they cope well with dryness and need only infrequent watering, with many vine types among them that can be hung for display. Hoya have sweet star-shaped flowers that resemble blooms made of wax, with many species being aromatic. Dischidia also have small red or white flowers. If cared for and soil conditions are good, the flowers can be enjoyed several times a year. Hoyas spread their stems out vigorously in all directions, while Dischidias grow by extending their leaves to trail downward.

Hoya kerrii 'Variegata'

Hoya carnosa "Variegata"
Country of origin: Cultivar
(Tropical Asia)

Hoya China bean
Country of origin: China, Nepal, India

Hoya caudata
Country of origin: Indonesia, Thailand, Malaysia

Hoya kerrii "Variegata"
Country of origin: Thailand, Laos

Hoya retusa
Country of origin: Tropical Asia

Dischidia emerald
Country of origin: South-east Asia

Dischidia ruscifolia
Country of origin: Asia, Oceania

Hoya Golden Eye
Country of origin: Borneo

TYPE: LEAFY PLANTS

Marantaceae

This family is characterized by the large variation of leaf color depending on the variety, as well as unique markings that resemble pictures on the leaves. Many varieties are colored differently on the surface and the reverse of the leaves, creating magnificent contrasts. New shoots emerge as tubular forms in warm environments and spread out, with cute flowers also blossoming. Many varieties have leaves which spread out during the day and stand upright to rest at night. This is in order to prevent the transpiration of water from the leaves, and is caused not only by light but also from the drying of the soil, strong winds and so on.

Calathea ornata
Country of origin: (Tropical America)

Calathea orbifolia
Country of origin: Tropical America

Calathea Beauty Star
Country of origin: Tropical America

Calathea Flamestar
Country of origin: Tropical America

Stromanthe Triostar
Country of origin: Cultivar (Tropical America)

Maranta leuconeura fasciata
Country of origin: Brazil

Calathea warscewiczii
Country of origin: Tropical America

Calathea lancifolia
Country of origin: Brazil

Calathea lancifolia

Polypodiaceae

The Japanese species name (uraboshi-ka = "reverse star" family) is derived from the star-like spores that cover the reverse sides of the leaves, which is one of the characteristics of this species. The reason that many of these plants are not only planted in pots but also mounted on boards or made into kokedama (moss balls) is that most types are epiphytes. It is popular to hang varieties such as the staghorn fern (*Platycerium bifurcatum*) with its deer antler-shaped sporophylls and *Aglaomorpha coronans* with its unique leaf shapes from the ceiling or on walls. New buds form in the growth period from spring to summer. Care for plants in this family by maintaining adequate moisture levels and keeping them out of direct sunlight in a place where air circulates well.

Microsorum musifolium

Platycerium bifurcatum cv. Netherlands
Country of origin: Cultivar (Tropical Asia)

Phlebodium aureum Blue Star
Country of origin: Tropical Asia

Microsorum musifolium
Country of origin: South-east Asia, Oceania

Platycerium veitchii
Country of origin: Australia

Aglaomorpha coronans
Country of origin: South-east Asia

Asparagaceae

Has a cool, masculine appearance and many fanciers. There are also many cultivars, with new varieties being created all the time. The air purifying Sansevieria and the Agave, known as the base ingredient for tequila, are popular species typical of this family. As they store water in their fleshy leaves, they are resilient against dryness, and if grown in pots, their growth speed slows. Sansevieria flower from spring to summer, while Agave flower only once every few decades. Once Agave bloom, the plant stock dies.

Sansevieria Boncellensis

Agave desmettiana
Country of origin: Mexico

Agave desmettiana

Agave attenuata
Country of origin: Mexico

Sansevieria kirkii var. pulchra "Coppertone"
Country of origin: Tropical Africa

Sansevieria bacularis
Country of origin: Africa

Sansevieria Masoniana Variegata
Country of origin: Tropical Africa

Agave potatorum
Country of origin: Mexico

Sansevieria Boncellensis
Country of origin: Africa, South Asia

Agave x "Blue Emperor"
Country of origin: Cultivar (Mexico)

Asteraceae

Popular as a succulent, *Senecio rowleyanus* (green necklace) grows as a vine, with its stems and leaves growing and trailing down, so can be enjoyed placed on a shelf or as a hanging pot. From early spring through to summer when the weather warms, it has many small flowers. There are many types, such as *variegata*, *radicans*, peach and ruby, with *peregrinus* (dolphin necklace) popular all over the world for its leaves that resemble a chain of dolphins jumping. Look out particularly for moldering in the rainy season and root rot in the heat and high humidity of summer.

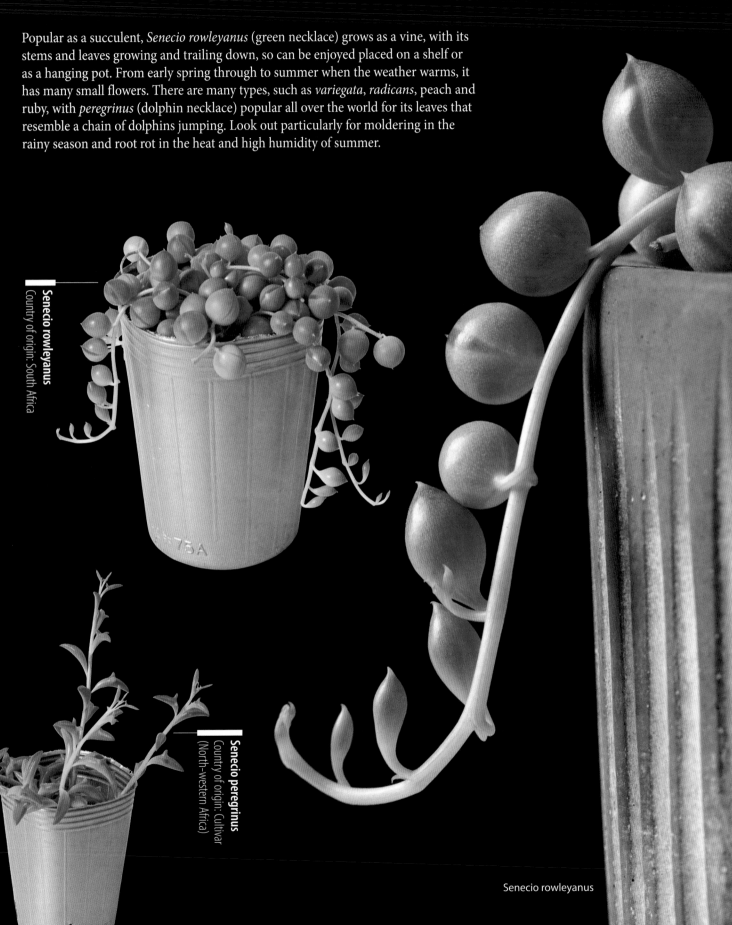

Senecio rowleyanus
Country of origin: South Africa

Senecio peregrinus
Country of origin: Cultivar
(North-western Africa)

Senecio rowleyanus

Aloidendron dichotomum

Xanthorrhoeaceae

Depending on the variety, the extremely popular Haworthia can fetch very high prices. Obtusa, with its leaves that are beautiful and drop-like when held up to the light, grows by letting light in through transparent "windows" or lenses in the leaves and blooms from spring to early summer. Pups emerge at the side of the plant to increase the stock. Apply the same cautions as per Asteraceae when cultivating these plants. Said to be the largest of the aloes, *Aloidendron dichotomum* has smooth skin on its trunk that when touched, conveys a sense of the plant's growth history. It is said to reach heights of more than 10m in its native habitat.

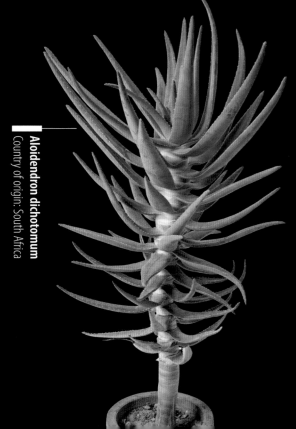

Aloidendron dichotomum
Country of origin: South Africa

Haworthia obtusa
Country of origin: South Africa

TYPE: SUCCULENTS AND CACTI

Crassulaceae

Characterized by fleshy leaves and stems that can store water.
Popular since long ago, *Crassula ovata* (jade plant) has adorable
pale pink flowers in winter. Keep it in a bright spot all year round
and reduce watering in fall to ensure it flowers well. Popular for its
glossy blackish purple color, *Aeonium arboreum* cv. *Atropurpureum*
grows new stock from its stem that creates the appearance of flowers
blooming. It is dormant over summer, having the qualities of plants
with winter growth periods for the rest of the year, so its new growth
can be enjoyed in the winter when other plants are not active.

Aeonium arboreum cv. Atropurpureum

Aeonium arboreum cv. Atropurpureum
Country of origin: Cultivar (Mediterranean coast)

Crassula ovata
Country of origin: South Africa

TYPE: SUCCULENTS AND CACTI

Lamiaceae

Lamiaceae includes aromatic varieties with essential oils in their leaves that are widely enjoyed as herbs. Aromaticus is a succulent herb with adorable round leaves that release a fresh fragrance when pressed between the fingers. Apart from having a deodorizing effect, it can be enjoyed in food and drinks and can also be used in the bath. New shoots emerge from the tips of the leaves, partway along the stem and from the base of the stock, so pick them off at the edges as they grow. During the growth period, if the leaves become too dense they will yellow and drop off so remove the petioles.

Aromaticus
Country of origin: South-east Asia, India, South Africa

Euphorbiaceae

Native to the tropics of south-east Asia, South America and Africa, these succulents include varieties with extremely unique forms and appearances and are growing in popularity as interior plants. Among them is the must-see Euphorbia platyclada, known as the zombie plant, which grows with reddish-brown leaves that give it a dead look. Another plant not to be missed is the oncoclada, which has long, slender foliage. In early spring when it gets warm, most types blossom with small flowers, and it's possible to enjoy the contrast of the unusual plant stock and lovely flowers.

Euphorbia acrurensis
Country of origin: Tropical Africa

Euphorbia oncoclada f. crist
Country of origin: Madagascar

Euphorbia oncoclada f. crist

Euphorbia platyclada
Country of origin: Madagascar

Euphorbia tirucalli
Country of origin: East Africa

Euphorbia lactea "White Ghost"
Country of origin: Cultivar (India)

Euphorbia milii (crown of thorns)
Country of origin: Madagascar

Euphorbia lactea
Country of origin: India

Euphorbia Sotetsukirin (pineapple cone)
Country of origin: Cultivar
(South Africa)

Cactaceae

Succulent plants native to North and Central America. The difference between cacti and other succulents is that cacti have spine pads (white fluffy parts with spines). Multiple spines grow from these, but some degenerate. Cacti have various appearances depending on their variety, such as column types, cord types and spherical types. In the growth period from spring to fall, keep them in a warm, bright place and water when the soil has dried out. In the dormant period over winter, reduce watering. Creating a well-balanced rhythm in care over the year will improve flowering.

Cereus peruvianus
Country of origin: Cultivar (Brazil, Uruguay)

Consolea rubescens
Country of origin: West Indies

Cereus peruvianus

Rhipsalis puniceo discus
Country of origin: South Africa

Rhipsalis Cassutha
Country of origin: Tropical Africa, Sri Lanka etc

Rhipsalis cereuscula
Country of origin: South Africa

Rhipsalis ewaldiana
Country of origin: South Africa

Hildewintera colademononis
Country of origin: Central to South America

Epiphyllum anguliger
Country of origin: Central to South America

TYPE: SUCCULENTS AND CACTI

Cucurbitaceae

Vines that are distributed widely throughout the tropics. The Green Drum succulent is typical as a house plant. Its common name comes from its round, thick leaves resembling drums. They are often seen in hanging pots, but in their native growing environments they can grow as shrubs, reaching heights of up to a yard/ meter. Growth is slow, with small, pale yellow-green flowers blooming at the start of spring when the weather warms. The leaves grow upwards when the plant is relatively small, and then start to trail down as the plant grows and foliage increases and becomes heavier.

PART 4

Living with House Plants

This is basic knowledge for living with plants. For living things, daily care is essential. Here, we detail how to live with plants all year round. We have used photographs to explain pruning methods that are considered difficult. Additionally, from page 92 we have listed actual questions received in-store, so if you notice any unusual changes in your plants, please refer to these.

Basic Watering

Watering is a daily task and one of the important elements of care for plants. Done well, watering will lead to robust growth in plants. Understand the meaning of watering and pay attention to plants' signals to carry out watering suited to each plant.

About watering

Basic watering entails the soil completely drying out all the way to the center of the pot, then watering all the soil evenly until water flows out from the base of the pot. In order to confirm the dryness of the soil, use your fingers to test its moistness once the color of the soil surface has got paler, check whether the pot has got lighter in weight and so on. As the soil dries out, insects, fungus (including expired air), and waste products from root respiration accumulate in the soil air layer. Watering the soil when it is in this condition allows waste products to be flushed out along with the water from the hole in the base of the pot and replenishes the soil with clean water and air. The oxygen necessary for roots to breathe is also provided through watering. The key point is to make sure all the soil receives plenty of water. Water that has accumulated in the dish beneath the pot contains waste products, so make sure to throw it out. The faster this cycle of "drying" "watering" and "removing waste products" is repeated, the better the growing environment for the plant. Too much soil can cause the roots to not dry out and suffocate (root rot), with the soil becoming unhealthy because waste products are not removed and new oxygen does not enter the soil. It's also important to choose a planter that is the right size for the plant.

Key tips for watering

As plants use stored water for activity during the day, water in the morning. Additionally, use a spray bottle to mist the surface and reverse of the leaves. This improves the growing environment and controls pests and fungus. Leaf watering can be carried out multiple times per day, so do it diligently.

Soil drying makes roots grow

When soil dries, roots grow to seek water. In order to create good stock with firm roots, it's important to balance wet and dry soil. Furthermore, soil dries at different intervals in the hot summer and cold winter, so carefully observe conditions and water accordingly.

How to Prevent Plants from Dying

Regardless of whether you choose a robust variety, if not cared for, a plant will gradually get weaker. Unlike when growing in the ground, growing in planters and plant pots creates harsh conditions for plants. These are four tips for preventing plants dying.

1. Don't decide the frequency and amount of water arbitrarily

We sometimes hear of people growing plants by giving them a cup of water each weekend, irrespective of the plant type, but this kind of approach is to be avoided. Follow the watering methods on p80 and give the necessary amount of water at the necessary time.

2. The basic rule is to keep plants indoors! Only place outdoors in spring and fall

Ornamental plants are for growing indoors. If left outdoors for long periods of time in midsummer or midwinter, their leaves will be damaged by direct sunlight or cold, and the stock may be fatally damaged, causing the plant to die. The recommended climate for outdoor exposure is 70°–85 °F / 20°–30 °C, out of direct sunlight.

3. Avoid unnecessary replanting

If replanting is not carried out in the appropriate season or with the right timing, it can damage the stock (see p88). Don't replant simply because "the plant didn't seem healthy so I just decided to" or "I always replant things as soon as I buy them, regardless of the time of year." In particular, replanting weakened stock can be fatal to the plant.

4. Observe carefully

Daily observation of the plant's condition is crucial for it to live a long life. Carefully observe the plant's condition to check whether there are insects clinging to it, the leaves are facing down and turning yellow and so on. The quicker you notice these things, the quicker you can take measures against them and maintain the health of the plant.

Basic Tools

Tools needed at a bare minimum are listed under "Necessary tools," while those to acquire if you can afford them are listed under "Handy tools". Be sure to get the "necessary tools" at the same time as purchasing the plants, and add to them afterward as required.

NECESSARY TOOLS

Spray bottle
Use for watering leaves. The fine mist type is also recommended.

Gardening scissors
Use for care such as pruning and so on.

Watering can
There are all kinds of designs, so choose one to suit your taste. Ones with narrow spouts are handy.

Gardening gloves
Protect your hands while handling soil, during tasks such as replanting and so on.

Shovel/soil scoop
Use for replanting, adding soil and so on.

Shallow dish (saucer)
Dish to catch water flowing from the base of the pot.

HANDY TOOLS

Moisture meter
Measures the moisture content in soil to let you know when to water.

Plant trolley
Handy for moving heavy pots. There are many designs available.

Automatic plant watering device
Does the watering for you when you're away. Poke into a water bottle to use.

Grow light
Enables plants to grow even in dark places.

Towel
For wiping leaves and pots. Make one to use for plants.

Soil for ornamental plants
Use for replanting or when soil levels are low.

Newspaper
Place under plants when replanting or carrying out other care indoors.

Pot cover
Choose something stylish to match your décor and that works with the plant.

Thermo-hygrometer
Use to measure optimal temperature and humidity for plants.

Mulching material
A décor material to conceal soil. It raises humidity levels so remove for two days after watering.

Basics of Fertilizer Use

Even if plants seem to have lost their vigor, blindly applying fertilizer can cause stock to weaken. Make sure to have a good understanding of fertilizer and use it correctly. Refer to instructions on the usage methods and amounts for the fertilizer purchased.

About fertilizers

When it comes to fertilizers, remember "type" and "season". Broadly speaking, there are two types. One is "fertilizer," which contains the three major elements necessary for plants to live: nitrogen (N), phosphoric acid (P) and potassium (K), while the other is "vitalizer," which has activating components apart from the three major elements as its main ingredients. In contrast to fertilizer, which is used for plant growth, vitalizer is designed to make plants grow robust and without troubles occurring. If compared with human food, fertilizer is a staple like bread or vegetables, while vitalizer is a supplementary food like fruit, supplements or energy drinks. Vitalizer used alone lacks nutrients, so should be used in combination with fertilizer. They should be administered together during the growth period from spring to fall. Do not give them to plants in midsummer, midwinter, directly after replanting or when the plant's condition is poor. Refer to each individual fertilizer in terms of how much to administer. The ratio of the three major elements—nitrogen, phosphoric acid and potassium —are always listed on fertilizer packages. Nitrogen is for leaves, phosphoric acid for fruit and flowers and potassium for roots.

TYPICAL FERTILIZERS AND HOW TO USE THEM

[Note: The fertilizers and vitalizers shown here are organic. There are many organic and non-organic brands and forms available. Be sure to research the needs of your particular plants before you buy these supplements, and always follow the manufacturers' instructions.]

■ These are two liquid options— nutrient-rich and suitable for all types of indoor plants. Add small amounts to water as directed, and water as usual.

■ These are two examples of time-release solid fertilizer options. They're a good choice if you prefer to fertilize infrequently or would like a more gradual addition of nutrients to the soil.

■ Vitalizing supplements like these are designed to replenish minerals in the soil, aid in water uptake, enhance growth and boost immunity. There are many of these on the market, and each is intended to meet specific needs. When choosing, take into consideration your plants' requirements and whatever your soil might be lacking.

Four Environments that Plants Prefer

If you create the right environment, it won't be hard to cultivate healthy plants. As plants grow naturally outside, it is difficult to achieve exactly the same conditions indoors, but keep these four environments in mind.

Bright and sunny

If plants do not receive sunlight, they cannot perform photosynthesis and will not grow properly. Fluorescent light alone does not provide sufficient light, and as the wavelengths of this light are not suited to photosynthesis, plants grown under it will become spindly and lose their color. If growing plants somewhere dark, use a growth light.

Good airflow

As plants naturally grow outside, they do not like environments where air does not circulate. Forcing out stale air and allowing fresh air to circulate will help them to grow healthier. Open windows, use an air circulator and so on to create airflow.

High temperatures and humidity

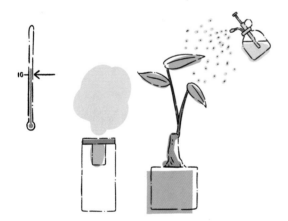

Most house plants grow natively in environments with high temperatures and humidity. Try as much as possible to recreate this environment when growing them. Avoid placing them anywhere that is less than 50 °F/ 10 °C the whole day through, and create humidity by using a spray bottle or humidifier. Direct breeze from air conditioners is extremely drying and is to be avoided at all costs.

Few changes in surroundings

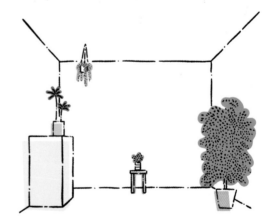

As plants naturally grow by rooting themselves to a spot and not moving, their condition will deteriorate from stress due to changes in surroundings if frequently moved from place to place. Apart from moving them to avoid heat and cold in midsummer and midwinter, once you have decided where to place them, keep them there rather than frequently shifting them around.

Points to Keep in Mind When Away from Home

Summer and winter vacations along with major holidays coincide with harsh times for plants, and it is not uncommon for them to die while you are away. These are the four tips to particularly keep in mind when away from home. However, if you will be gone for more than three days, it is necessary to ask someone to help out.

Don't let the water run out

It is not uncommon for soil to completely dry out while people are away from home, with all the plant's leaves shed on their return. Before you leave, make sure to check whether the soil has dried out and if it looks like it might dry out while you are gone, water the plant. Using an automatic watering device will put your mind at ease.

Keep temperature changes to a minimum

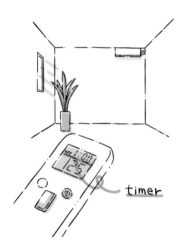

If closed rooms become extremely hot or cold, plants' roots become damaged and the plant will become limp. Use the timer on the air conditioner to adjust the temperature during the day in summer and in the morning and evening during winter. Additionally, place plants where they can get faint sunlight.

Prevent air from stagnating

If left for a long time in a closed room where air does not circulate, plants will suffer a great strain. Open doors to rooms, open ventilation openings and turn on the extraction fan.
If you have a circulator, switch it on to create airflow throughout the room.

Place plants outdoors during the hottest months

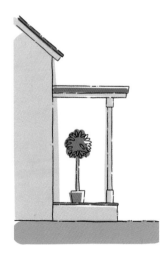

In the hottest period of summer, there are limits to what can be achieved indoors, regardless of the measures taken. If you have an outdoor space that does not get direct sunlight, move the plant there. As this prevents sudden changes in temperature and humidity, it decreases the risk of root damage.

Precautions for Summer and Winter

Midsummer and midwinter are the seasons in which the most caution is needed when cultivating plants. Big changes in heat and cold are very difficult for plants, and may cause leaf burn and so on. Here, we look at changes in the environment that tend to get overlooked in the course of daily life, along with points to be aware of in summer and winter.

Precautions for summer

Just as people get sunburnt from the sun's heat, plants left by a window with no filtering (such as curtains) or put outside even for a short time for watering can get leaf burn from the heat. Leaves that are burnt and have changed color will not revert back to their original color and need to be pruned off, so be very careful to avoid leaf burn. Furthermore, soil tends to dry out quickly in the summer heat, so make sure plants do not run out of water. It is best to carefully check the dryness of the soil regularly to prevent this. With regard to inadequate water, we often hear from people whose plants were fine in the morning, but have gone limp and droopy by the end of the work day. Even if there seems to be no change in a plant's appearance, careful inspection may reveal that the soil is completely dry, and the daytime heat has exhausted the plant. Make a habit of checking the dryness of the soil particularly in the morning over summer.

Precautions for winter

Take care with watering and watch out for dryness in the air. Watering should definitely be carried out indoors as placing plants outside in cold air even for the smallest amount of time can cause leaf burn and damage the stock. Additionally, plants actually often run dry over winter. Some people leave plants alone in the mistaken belief that winter is the dormant season, so they need to reduce watering, but the basic rule of giving plenty of water when soil has dried out does not change over winter. Once soil has dried out, water plants properly. If rooms are warm due to heating, it may be necessary to water as often as for the start of spring. Furthermore, dry air leads to dust and dirt settling on leaves, so wipe them often and water the leaves. If grime collects on the leaves, it will be difficult for the plant to perform photosynthesis and its energy levels will become depleted. Additionally, dry conditions and dirt create an environment conducive to spider mites. In winter, sunlight is weak and the sun does not shine for long, so plants lose energy. Efforts such as the above-mentioned are key to help them get through winter in good health.

Prevention and Countermeasures for Pests

The main inhibitors to plants' growth are pests and disease. The types of pests attracted and tendencies for disease differ depending on plant varieties, but the most common are listed here. The basic rule is to carefully observe plants and kill pests as soon as they are found. If that does not work, chemicals may be used.

Name : Scale insect

Symptom : Leaves and branches become sticky

Prevention/countermeasures: Regularly prune branches and leaves that are becoming dense in order to improve airflow. Use a toothbrush to brush insects off and apply chemicals.

Name : Spider mite

Symptoms : Leaves develop a patchy white appearance, with some like spiderwebs.

Prevention/countermeasures: Spray leaves with water to prevent infestations. If pests are found, wash the entire plant stock with water and apply chemicals once dry.

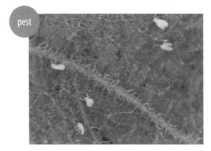

Name : Whitefly

Symptoms : Infest the backs of leaves, making the leaves a patchy white.

Prevention/countermeasures: Spray leaves with water to prevent infestations. If pests are found, wash the entire plant stock with water and apply chemicals once dry.

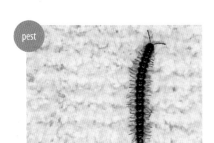

Name : Millipedes

Symptoms : Emerge from within the soil. May secrete an unpleasant odor.

Prevention/countermeasures: Pour water containing chemicals into a bucket and place the entire pot in it until it is semi submerged.

Name : Ants

Symptoms : Emerge from within the soil. If a nest is built it will weaken the entire plant.

Prevention/countermeasures: Control through the use of chemicals.

Name : Drosophilidae/Springtails

Symptoms : Emerge from within the soil. Troublesome when large numbers occur indoors.

Prevention/countermeasures: Dry soil out properly before watering. Do not use organic fertilizer. Akadama soil strewn on the soil surface is effective. Exterminate with an insecticide spray.

Name : Mildew

Symptoms : White spore-like fluffy material spreads over the soil surface

Prevention/countermeasures: Avoid high humidity and place in a spot that is guaranteed to get sunlight and good airflow. Remove soil and apply an alcohol spray.

Name : Anthrax

Symptoms : Blackish spots form on the leaves, eventually turning gray and drying out the leaves until they die.

Prevention/countermeasures: Regularly prune dense foliage to improve airflow. Cut off any leaves or branches affected.

Name : Brown spot

Symptoms : Brown spots form on the leaves and spread, with the leaves falling off.

Prevention/countermeasures: Regularly prune dense foliage to improve airflow. Cut off any leaves or branches affected.

Let's Replant

The first thing to do after purchasing a plant is replanting (repotting)*. Plants purchased as seedlings can also be planted using these steps. This is also an effective process if you want to make plants grow bigger and bigger. For plants, replanting is a stressful aspect of their care. Make sure you understand it properly before carrying it out.

*Some plants are sold in a good condition so ask at the time of purchase whether replanting is necessary.

Is replanting necessary?

If cultivating a plant in a plant pot, it is necessary to replant it regularly. The reason for this is that in order for the plant to grow healthily, it is necessary to maintain and nurture a good environment in the pot. The soil and roots are being cultivated in a limited space, so as time passes, roots grow and fill up the pot, causing the conditions to deteriorate and leading to poor growth. Once roots grow and become clogged, they are unable to absorb enough oxygen and minerals, causing the plant to die. Furthermore, as nutrients in the soil are absorbed by the roots along with water, they decrease as time passes. If such a situation continues, the plant will start to run into trouble, with leaf color fading, new shoots in good condition failing to sprout, leaves starting to drop and so on. This situation is improved through replanting. Carrying it out regularly creates healthy roots and good foliage, allowing an attractive appearance to be maintained.

This is when to replant!

Replanting is necessary when plant stock gets large and unstable, more than two years have passed since purchasing the plant, roots start emerging from the base of the pot, soil decreases and water runs out of the pot base as soon as the plant is watered, conversely also when water does not come out of the base of the pot regardless of how much is given*, and so on. If any of these apply, it is time to repot.

*As a guide, for plant pot sizes 3-6 water should run out within one minute, for sizes 7 and over, allow two minutes.

Replant in the growth period from spring to fall

May–September
60-86 °F/20-30 °C

Any time is fine!

Replanting is, in human terms, like having an operation, so do it during the growth period when plants have strength. Warm periods from May to September when temperatures are between 60–86 °F are ideal. Replanting in midsummer and midwinter or when the plant is not in good condition can cause planting damage, so avoid doing this.

The Replanting Process

1 TOOLS NEEDED

Ficus benjamina barok, soil, stones for the pot base, gloves, cloth for wiping, pot, shovel, mesh for pot base, disposable chopsticks, akadama soil (medium grain).

2

Place the mesh over the hole in the pot base and pour in stones over the top until they take up about 1/10 of the pot. (This is to improve drainage)

3

Pour soil in to conceal the stones, then add the plant to get an idea of its height in the pot. If the roots look as if they will be exposed, lightly loosen them at this point.

4

Add soil in to about an inch (2-3 cm) from the top of the pot (this will form the water space).

5

Use the disposable chopsticks to poke the soil in so that it reaches all the way into the center. When doing this, make sure not to damage the roots by pressing in around the edge of the pot.

6

Lift the pot slightly every so often and lightly let it drop in order to settle the soil into the pot.

7

Once the soil is in place, use the pads of your fingers to press the plant stock in and stabilize it so it doesn't shift around.

8

Lastly, strew the akadama soil on top. (It plays a cosmetic role and also prevents insects)

9

Water until water runs out of the pot base to complete the planting. Do not fertilize until the roots have settled after replanting (around two weeks).

Let's Prune (Adjusting the Form of a Plant)

The process of trimming off branches and leaves is called pruning, and for plants cultivated in plant pots, it is a task that cannot be avoided. It is a relatively difficult process, so get an understanding of it and prune according to each plant's needs. Pruning creates vigorous, attractive growth in plants.

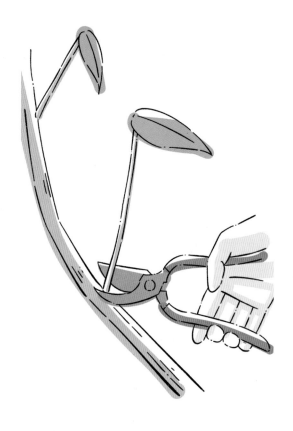

What is pruning?

Pruning is the process of cutting unwanted or dead branches and leaves to improve air circulation. It is a necessary task in order for plants to grow vigorously and attractively for a long time. Creating good air circulation is crucial for cultivating healthy plants, but when plants are grown over a long time, leaves and branches become overgrown and crowd each other. This creates poor circulation and an environment conducive to infestations of pests. It is possible to prevent pests through regular pruning. Furthermore, pruning makes the flow of nutrients from the roots to new buds and existing foliage more effective, making it easier for the plants to produce new leaves. It also allows the shape and form of the plant to be adjusted and tidied so that it can maintain an attractive appearance. Pruning is best done in the period from May to July. If done in cold periods it can damage the plant so is to be avoided. In high humidity, cuts do not dry properly, making it easier for bacteria and mold to take hold, so make sure to prune on dry, fine days.

Prune boldly

Some people don't prune for years as they feel sorry for cutting off leaves and branches that have grown so long, but pruning is necessary for regeneration when cultivating plants in pots, so take the plunge and give it a go. The new buds that emerge after pruning are adorable!

Pruning precautions

Sap emerges from the cuts in some plants when they are pruned, and if the sap of some varieties is touched, such as plants in the Araceae family or types of Ficus, it can cause a rash. Wear gloves and make sure not to touch sap directly as you work.

The Pruning Process

1 TOOLS NEEDED

Gardening scissors, gloves

2

A Syzygium cumini prior to pruning. Many new buds have emerged, creating an over-grown look. Prune the plant to make it neat and improve air circulation.

3

Broadly visualize the overall form of the plant after pruning and make a start. Commercially available plants are often cut at the growth point* of the main trunk, so there is basically no problem with cutting any part of the growing branches and leaves.

*The part of a plant at the root or stem end where cell division takes place.

4

When cutting, cut directly above the leaf. New buds will emerge from just below the cut, so this will improve the form of the plant once they grow.

5

There's no need to cut on the diagonal as you would for cut flowers—cut straight across.

6

As this tree shape is attractive when the trunk can be seen from front-on, prune off the over-grown sections from the base up.

7

For branches growing in the same direction, steadily cut bit by bit off the longest branch.

8

Prune off and fine-tune areas of concern in particular sections.

9

Completion of pruning. Dense areas have been reduced, creating good airflow. Think of pruning like a haircut, and cut off steadily bit by bit. In general, visualize taking off about $\frac{1}{3}$ of the total volume of the plant when pruning.

Frequently Asked Questions

Here are some of the questions we're often asked at Green Interior.
If your plant displays unusual characteristics, we hope you'll find a solution below.

Question   The leaves of the plant are sticky…

Answer — It's possible that the plant may be infested with scale insect. There are various forms, such as a pill bug-like kind covered with a hard brown shell, and some with a white cottony shape. These insects are one of the most common of those found on house plants. They hide in places where they are difficult to find, on the backs of leaves and in the gaps between branches, leaving a sticky excrement. Rub them off using something such as a toothbrush, or if not possible to remove them in that way, use a special chemical agent in spray form. Using granule-type chemicals that can be spread on the soil to control the disease will help prevent recurrence.

Question   The ends of the leaves are going brown.

Answer — This is a phenomenon often seen in palms and Dracaena, and is caused by dryness in the air and a lack of water. Increase the frequency of watering and mist the plant frequently. Plants may be affected by strong sunlight in midsummer or the breeze from the air conditioner, so recheck how much sun and breeze they are getting. Cut off any sections that have turned brown with the scissors on a diagonal angle.

Question   The leaf color seems to be fading.

Answer — This may possibly be due to spider mites, which attach as parasites to the backs of leaves and such out the nutrients. The sections affected lose their chlorophyll, and the leaf as a whole takes on a whitish appearance. Spider mites are hard to see, but the foliage will feel dusty and rough to the touch and leave a brown soot-like substance on the fingers. As spider mites increase rapidly, they need to be exterminated by washing the entire plant stock in water, then wiping it and applying a chemical spray. Multiple applications are effective.

Question   There are a lot of small insects flying around the pot.

Answer — This may be an infestation of Drosophilidae emerging from the soil. Drosophilidae hide in a layer an inch or so (2-3 cm) below the soil and hatch in response to moisture, emerging on top of the soil. They will come out from the soil 1-2 minutes after watering, so spray a horticultural insecticide directly onto them. If you don't have any insecticide for horticultural use, a regular mosquito and fly spray is fine, but make sure to spray more than 8" (20 cm) away from the leaves and trunk of the plant. The flies' eggs may remain in the soil, so remove the top inch (2-3 cm) of the soil surface and discard it, replenishing the reduced soil with ornamental soil or akadama. As flies tend to infest soil with moisture content and nutrients, they often appear after replanting. Prevent this by avoiding placing mulch on top of the soil continuously and improving air circulation.

Question   Is it OK to cut overgrown leaves and branches?

Answer   Definitely prune the plant. Regularly pruning off old or unwanted branches makes it easier for new buds to form. Pruning is best carried out during the growth periods of spring and summer, focusing on removing withered branches, overgrown, straggly branches and dense growth. Prune by visualizing allowing ⅓ of the branches and leaves to remain. Unlike with garden trees, if pruning is carried out at the right time of year, even if a branch is cut off by mistake, it will not wither and die. (For types of palm, there is no problem cutting off the base of the leaves, but as the growth point is at the tip of the trunk, cutting it will cause the plant to wither and die, so care is needed.)

Question   The trunk is leaning to one side—what should I do?

Answer   As the stock grows and the top grows heavier, or soil thins out and decreases, the plant may start to lean. If it is the replanting season of spring or fall, bring the roots out from the plant pot and straighten them out to replant. If the pot seems too small, go one size up. If it is not the season for re-planting, use supports to reinforce the plant and add more soil to keep the plant firmly in place. If the weight of the foliage is causing the lean and it is the plant's growth period, carry out pruning as well.

Question   I can't put a plant in a cold entrance way or in the bathroom, can I?

Answer   That can be problematic. If plants don't get sunlight, airflow and the appropriate temperature, they will not grow properly and will eventually die. If you really want to display plants as part of the décor, we recommend doing so by normally keeping them in a bright spot and moving them indoors only when you have visitors, using artificial flowers and so on.

Question   I want a plant that stays the same size.

Answer   Plants are living things, so although the speed at which they grow varies, they will get bigger bit by bit. Prune the plant to keep it at a size that is easy to display.

Question   My plant has lost all its leaves. Is it still alive?

Answer   If all the leaves have fallen off, it's highly likely that root damage or lack of water could be the cause. Touch the trunk and if it is stiff and wrinkled, it is possibly still alive because water is still passing through it. Conversely, if it has whitened and dried out or turned black and gone soft, it is in a severe con-dition. If there are attractive pale green buds still remaining on the ends of the branches, there's no need to worry. Recovery from root damage is difficult, but if the plant has run out of water, new buds often start sprouting again once watering is resumed. Start by observing the condition of the trunk in order to assess the situation.

Question   The lower leaves of my Dracaena turn brown. Is it OK?

Answer   Dracaena put out new buds from the center of the plant stock, with the old lower leaves turn-ing brown and dropping off. This is normal regeneration so there is no need for concern. Once the leaves turn brown, cut them off at their base.

Question There seems to be something white, like mold, on the soil…

Answer It is probably mold, so remove it. As it is a bacteria, it may remain in the surrounding areas. Continue to observe the soil and if you find mold, remove it. It forms easily if soil is constantly moist or if the airflow above the soil is not good.

Question Fungi are growing with the plant…

Answer Fungi will not adversely affect the plant directly, but remove them. Similarly to dealing with mold, continue to observe the situation and if you find more fungi, remove them. They tend to grow if soil is constantly moist or if the airflow above the soil is not good.

Question The plant's leaf color is fading.

Answer This may be due to insufficient sunlight or root damage. Make sure the plant is getting the right amount of sunlight. If it is too dark, move the plant to somewhere as bright as possible. In the case of root damage, the trunk and stems will start turning black. Stop watering and wait until the soil dries out completely before giving the plant more water. When doing this, feel the soil or lift the plant pot to feel its weight in order to assess whether the soil has dried all the way through.

Question The plant is flowering. What should I do?

Answer After you have enjoyed the flowers for a while, prune the plant. If allowed to blossom, the plant will use energy and the leaves may turn yellow and fall off. It's also good to fertilize after flowering.

Question My succulent has "dissolved." What is the reason?

Answer This may occur if water is poured onto the plant stock or it is left in a hot bay window where air is trapped. When watering, make sure to only pour water onto the soil. If the plant stock is covering the soil, fill a bowl or vessel with water and sit the plant pot in it until half submerged to allow the water to be absorbed via the pot base. After about 30 minutes, the plant pot should be heavy with the water it has absorbed. Succulents often will not grow well if they do not receive good airflow in their growing environment, so make sure the plant gets some breeze occasionally.

Question After repotting, the plant stock became droopy and lost its vitality.

Answer It's possible that the roots were damaged during replanting or that it was not planted properly and is not able to absorb water. Spring and fall are the seasons for replanting, as roots can be damaged in the heat of midsummer or cold of midwinter. Furthermore, if soil is not firmly packed in around roots when replanted, they become unable to absorb water and the plant will become limp. Use something such as a stick to poke soil into the edges of the pot when replanting to make sure it reaches the bottom of the pot properly, then add soil and pat it down firmly. Even if a plant has lost vitality after repotting, replanting it again and giving it fertilizer will only damage it further, so don't do this. Allow it to recover in a warm, well-ventilated place.

Question   Spots are forming on the leaves and the leaves are falling off.

Answer   This may be caused by overwatering, keeping the plant somewhere dark, the leaves touching a wall, the foliage becoming too dense and so on. Check if any of these could apply. If the plant is kept next to a wall or in the corner of a room, the leaves on the side next to the wall don't tend to get light or breeze, so their condition will deteriorate. Rotate the plant occasionally and shift it slightly away from the wall; doing this should settle it down.

Question   I have a foliage plant; the whole plant is limp and drooping.

Answer   If the leaves and base of the plant stock are blackened and soft, it is root damage. It is often difficult to revive the plant in these situations. If the leaves have yellowed, or if they are their usual color but have gone limp, it's likely due to the soil having dried out. Use newspaper and lift the leaves up, wrapping the entire plant stock to form a conical shape. Pour water into a bowl and place the plant pot in it so it is half submerged, so the water enters the pot from the base. Once the pot has become heavy, remove it from the bowl and monitor the plant's condition. In most cases, the leaves lift up again in half a day to a day's time.

Question   What should I do about leaves that have gone yellow and developed spots?

Answer   If it is the growth period from spring to fall, prune the plant. If it is winter, the plant will not have any energy so try to refrain from pruning until spring.

Question   I have put plants in the same place several times, but they've all died.

Answer   There may be a problem with the place they are kept. Check again whether this place receives light, whether air can circulate, and whether the way you are watering is suitable. Furthermore, some plants like bright places whereas others prefer semi-shade. It might be a good idea to ask your local specialist store for advice.

Question   I want to grow plants, but my children are young and I'm worried they'll knock the pots over.

Answer   We recommend plants that can be hung from walls or suspended from the ceiling. Additionally, even placing small pots on shelves that cannot be reached can completely change the atmosphere of a room. Air plants that don't require soil are also good.

Question   The pot that my plant is in looks small. Is it OK not to use a bigger pot?

Answer   As long as there are no thick roots coming out from the base of the pot, it's fine to leave it as it is. For plants grown in plant pots, the faster the cycle of "soil drying out," "watering" and "rinsing away waste products," the better the growth environment, so the theory is that they should be able to be cultivated in pots that are not particularly large. If there is too much soil, it won't dry out well, lengthening the time before watering and leading to problems such as root rot.

Published by Tuttle Publishing,
an imprint of Periplus Editions (HK) Ltd.

www.tuttlepublishing.com

INTERIOR GREEN (Boutique Mook no.1544)
Copyright © 2021 GREEN INTERIOR, Boutique-sha, Inc.
English translation rights arranged with Boutique-sha, Inc.
through Japan UNI Agency, Inc., Tokyo
English Translation © 2023 by Periplus Editions (HK) Ltd.
Translated from Japanese by Leeyong Soo

ISBN 978-0-8048-5596-9

STAFF

Editorial supervision	Tomiya Chizuru
Editing	100nichi
Photography	Kitamura Yusuke
Book design	Miura Shuuko
Illustrations	Xian Ozn

Distributed by
North America, Latin America & Europe
Tuttle Publishing
364 Innovation Drive
North Clarendon, VT 05759-9436 U.S.A.
Tel: 1 (802) 773-8930
Fax: 1 (802) 773-6993
info@tuttlepublishing.com
www.tuttlepublishing.com

Japan
Tuttle Publishing
Yaekari Building 3rd Floor
5-4-12 Osaki
Shinagawa-ku
Tokyo 141-0032
Tel: (81) 3 5437-0171
Fax: (81) 3 5437-0755
sales@tuttle.co.jp
www.tuttle.co.jp

Asia Pacific
Berkeley Books Pte. Ltd.
3 Kallang Sector #04-01
Singapore 349278
Tel: (65) 6741 2178
Fax: (65) 6741 2179
inquiries@periplus.com.sg
www.tuttlepublishing.com

26 25 24 23   8 7 6 5 4 3 2 1
Printed in China   2301EP

TUTTLE PUBLISHING® is a registered trademark of Tuttle Publishing, a division of Periplus Editions (HK) Ltd.

House plant specialist store Green Interior
Working with the concept of "spreading the joy of living with
plants in daily life", the store proposes greenery's appeal as décor.
In addition to stocking ornamental plants from all over the world,
the store offers various after-sale services.

Sato Momoko
Sato Momoko studied systems, plants and landscaping at a
residential building company before joining Green Interior. She
oversees all aspects of the store from store branding to coordi-
nation and construction. When not devoting herself to Green
Interior, she enjoys visiting mountains and cooking.

Mashimo Yoshihiro
Having a deep interest in plants, Mashiko Yoshihiro visits
production areas throughout Japan and welcomes a wide variety
of plants into the store. After gaining experience at a wholesale
potted plant market and flower store, he joined Green Interior
at the time it launched. He was formerly a techno DJ.

"Books to Span the East and West"

Tuttle Publishing was founded in 1832 in the small
New England town of Rutland, Vermont [USA].
Our core values remain as strong today as they were
then—to publish best-in-class books which bring
people together one page at a time. In 1948, we
established a publishing outpost in Japan—and Tuttle
is now a leader in publishing English-language books
about the arts, languages and cultures of Asia. The
world has become a much smaller place today and
Asia's economic and cultural influence has grown. Yet
the need for meaningful dialogue and information
about this diverse region has never been greater. Over
the past seven decades, Tuttle has published thou-
sands of books on subjects ranging from martial arts
and paper crafts to language learning and literature—
and our talented authors, illustrators, designers and
photographers have won many prestigious awards.
We welcome you to explore the wealth of information
available on Asia at **www.tuttlepublishing.com.**